JUST **4** KIDS

JUST **4** KIDS

Love Food ® is an imprint of
Parragon Books Ltd

Parragon
Queen Street House
4 Queen Street
Bath BA1 1HE, UK

Love Food ® and the accompanying heart
device is a trade mark of Parragon Books Ltd

Design: Terry Jeavons & Company

ISBN 978-1-4075-3391-9

Printed in China

This book uses imperial, metric, and US cup
measurements. Follow the same units of
measurement throughout; do not mix imperial
and metric. All spoon measurements are level,
unless otherwise stated: teaspoons
are assumed to be 5ml, and tablespoons
are assumed to be 15ml. Unless otherwise
stated, milk is assumed to be whole-fat, eggs
and individual fruits, such as bananas, are
medium, and pepper is freshly ground
black pepper.

Recipes using raw or very lightly cooked eggs
should be avoided by children, the elderly,
pregnant women, convalescents, and anyone
with an illness. Pregnant and breast-feeding
women are advised to avoid eating peanuts
and peanut products.

Contents

Introduction 6

1 Breakfast 8

2 Meat & Poultry 36

3 Fish & Seafood 64

4 Vegetables 92

5 Snacks 120

6 Treats 148

Index 176

Introduction

If you find it a challenge to get your children to eat good, home-cooked food, then *Just 4 Kids* is the answer. With recipes specially written with children in mind, the book is an indispensable guide to making food that children will actually eat. Many of the recipes will appeal to adults, too, because today's busy lifestyles mean that there is rarely time to cook separately and children's meals are the family's meals. For parents at home with children, the book contains plenty of ideas for attractive dishes to tempt babies and toddlers, as well as more sophisticated fare for older siblings.

The book begins with breakfast, the most important meal of the day and the one that is often the most difficult to get school-age children to eat. The recipes have been chosen to tempt children in a hurry or with little appetite, but there are also substantial dishes for those who start the day feeling ravenous.

Meat, poultry, and fish are vital for growing children and teenagers. The recipes include a fantastic selection of tasty dishes from around the world, guaranteed to satisfy all ages and appetites. The vegetable recipes ingeniously combine mildly flavored or sweet-tasting varieties with ingredients such as beans and pasta, so your children will hardly know they are eating them. The recipes are also perfect if you have a vegetarian in the family.

There is an all-important chapter devoted to healthy snacks, both sweet and savory. The trick is to have snacks ready when needed, so your children will be less likely to demand sugary sweets and drinks. Sandwich fillings and dips, such as hummus, can be made in advance and stored in the refrigerator. Popcorn and nachos can be made in minutes and are fun for children to help with. The book finishes with a wonderful selection of delicious treats that your children will love, whether it's baked rice dessert for everyday eating, or a spectacular sundae for a special occasion.

When time is short, it often seems easier to opt for packaged convenience foods. However, there is no denying that food freshly prepared at home is likely to be better for your children and the rest of the family, too. By making food from scratch, you know exactly what's going into it and you can plan meals so that your children get the most nutritious food for their particular stage of physical development.

It's a good idea to encourage your children to help you in the kitchen. Involving them in a few simple tasks or letting them cook a recipe from start to finish (with a little parental guidance) will help develop a life-long interest in good wholesome food.

1 Breakfast

An energy-rich breakfast makes a nutritious start to the day, especially important for school-age children. Creamy oatmeal or muesli with nuts and dried fruit will keep energy levels stable until lunchtime, as will a cooked breakfast of scrambled or baked eggs. Chilled smoothies and yogurt are easy-to-eat options for those in a hurry. Fruity muffins or fruit-and-nut bread make a change from toast, and will be popular with all ages and tastes.

Fruity Purple Oatmeal

INGREDIENTS

serves ❹

3½ oz/100 g g fresh or defrosted frozen mixed berries

⅓ cup rolled oats

generous ⅓ cup milk

1–2 tsp honey (optional)

plain yogurt, to serve (optional)

1 Take half the fruit and process to a puree using a hand blender. Put the oats and milk into a small saucepan and simmer gently for about 5 minutes, stirring from time to time. Cool a little and stir in the honey, if using.

2 Pour into a serving bowl and stir in the fruit puree, making a swirling pattern. Roughly chop the remaining fruit and scatter on top. Serve with plain yogurt if liked.

Muesli Muffins

INGREDIENTS

3½ oz/100 g plumped dried apricots, chopped

4 tbsp orange juice

2 eggs

1¼ cups sour cream

3½ fl oz/100 ml sunflower oil

scant ½ cup light brown sugar

2 cups self-rising flour

1 tsp baking powder

TOPPING

¼ cup light brown sugar

⅓ cup crunchy muesli, lightly crushed

2 tbsp butter, melted

makes ❶❷ large or ❸❻ small muffins

1 Preheat the oven to 375°F/190°C.

2 Put the apricots and orange juice into a small bowl and let to soak for about 15 minutes. Put the eggs into a bowl and beat. Add the sour cream, oil, and sugar. Add the apricot mixture and stir well. Put the flour and baking powder into a bowl and gently stir in the egg and apricot mixture. Do not over-mix.

3 Spoon the mixture into paper cases in a muffin pan. Mix together the topping ingredients and sprinkle over the top of the muffins. Bake for about 10–15 minutes for small muffins and 25–30 for larger muffins.

Smoothies

INGREDIENTS

serves 2

FRUIT SMOOTHIE

½ mango, peeled and chopped

1 small banana

4–6 strawberries

scant ½ cup plain yogurt with added honey

⅔ cup milk

4 ice cubes

MALTED BANANA SMOOTHIE

1 small banana, chopped

scant 1 cup milk

2 tbsp malted milk powder

4 ice cubes

FRUIT SMOOTHIE

1 Put all the ingredients into a blender and process until smooth. Pour out and serve with straws.

MALTED BANANA SMOOTHIE

1 Put all the ingredients into a blender and process until smooth. To make a chocolate variation, use chocolate malted milk powder and chocolate ice cream. Pour out and serve with straws.

Coconut Muesli

INGREDIENTS

1⅓ cups rolled oats

3¾ cups wheat flakes

3 tbsp raisins

⅓ cup dried unsulfured apricots, finely chopped

½ cup roasted hazelnuts, finely chopped

⅓ cup dry unsweetened shredded coconut

freshly grated apple (optional)

milk, to serve

makes ⑩ portions

1 Mix together the oats, wheat flakes, raisins, apricots, hazelnuts, and coconut. Store the mixture in an airtight container.

2 Just before serving, mix a few spoonfuls of the muesli with 2 tablespoons of freshly grated apple, if liked, and serve with milk.

Baked Eggs

INGREDIENTS

butter, for greasing

2 large eggs

2 tbsp light cream

salt and pepper

serves ❷

1 Preheat the oven to 375°F/190°C. Generously butter 2 small ramekins and break 1 egg into each dish. Season well with salt and pepper and spoon over 1 tablespoon light cream.

2 Place the dishes in a roasting pan with enough hot water to come halfway up the sides of the dishes and bake for 15 minutes for a soft egg and 18–20 minutes for a firmer egg.

Blueberry Bran Muffins

INGREDIENTS

heaping 1 cup white all-purpose flour

scant ¾ cup whole wheat self-rising flour

1 tbsp oat bran

2 tsp baking powder

½ tsp baking soda

pinch of salt

¼ cup packed raw sugar

1 tbsp honey

1 large egg

scant 1 cup buttermilk

heaping 1¼ cups fresh blueberries

makes 10

1 Preheat the oven to 350°F/180°C. Line 10 holes of a muffin pan with muffin paper cases.

2 Mix the flours, bran, baking powder, baking soda, and salt together in a bowl and stir in the sugar. Whisk the honey, egg, and buttermilk together in a pitcher.

3 Pour the wet ingredients into the dry and stir briefly to combine. Don't overmix—the batter should still be a little lumpy. Fold in the blueberries.

4 Spoon the batter into the paper cases and bake in the preheated oven for 20 minutes, until risen and lightly browned.

5 Remove the muffins from the oven and let cool in the pan. Serve warm or cold.

Sunshine Toast

INGREDIENTS

serves ❶

1 slice whole wheat bread

1 tbsp olive oil

2–3 mushrooms, sliced

1 tomato, halved

1 small egg

pepper

1 Using a cookie cutter, cut a hole in the center of the slice of bread, large enough to hold the egg.

2 Heat the oil in a nonstick skillet and cook the mushrooms and tomato, cut-sides down, for 3–4 minutes, until the mushrooms are beginning to brown. Turn the tomato over.

3 Make a space in the middle of the skillet and add the bread. Crack the egg open and carefully pour it into the hole in the bread. Reduce the heat and cook slowly until cooked through.

4 Season everything to taste with pepper and serve the sunshine toast with the mushrooms and tomato alongside.

Crunchy Yogurt

INGREDIENTS

serves ❷

2⅓ cups rolled oats

2 tbsp honey

2 tbsp pumpkin seeds

2 tbsp sunflower seeds

2 tbsp chopped walnuts

1 small ripe pear, peeled, cored, and chopped

½ ripe mango, pitted, peeled, and chopped

generous ½ cup plain yogurt

1 Preheat the oven to 350°F/180°C.

2 Mix the oats and honey together in a bowl and spread out on a baking sheet. Bake in the preheated oven for 10–15 minutes, stirring a couple of times, until the oats are lightly browned, then remove from the oven and let cool.

3 Place the seeds in a mortar and briefly grind with a pestle to break them into smaller pieces. Mix with the cooled oats and the walnuts.

4 To assemble, put half the pear and mango in a glass and top with half the yogurt and a spoonful of granola. Repeat with the remaining fruit and yogurt and top with more granola.

Bircher Granola

INGREDIENTS

serves **4**

3 cups rolled oats

1 tbsp wheat germ

scant 1 cup whole milk or soy milk

2 tbsp honey, plus extra for serving (optional)

2 tbsp plain yogurt

1 apple, peeled, cored, and grated

1 cup chopped nuts, such as macadamia nuts, cashews, or hazelnuts

mixed berries, such as blueberries, raspberries, and strawberries

fruit puree, to serve (optional)

1 The night before serving, mix the oats, wheat germ, and milk together in a bowl, cover with plastic wrap, and let chill overnight.

2 To serve, stir the oat mixture, add the honey, yogurt, and apple, and mix well.

3 Spoon into serving bowls, top with the nuts and berries, and drizzle over a little more honey, or fruit puree, if using.

Apple & Hazelnut Bread

INGREDIENTS

makes ❶ loaf

butter, for greasing

1½ cups warm water

1 tsp golden superfine sugar

¼-oz/7-g packet active dry yeast

heaping 2¾ cups all-purpose flour, plus extra for dusting

heaping 2¾ cups light brown self-rising flour

½ tsp salt

heaping ¾ cup toasted hazelnuts, chopped

1¾ oz/50 g dried apple, chopped

1 apple, grated

TO SERVE

honey

sliced banana or nut butter

1 Grease and line an 8 x 4 x 2-inch/20 x 10 x 5-cm loaf pan. Put a generous ⅓ cup of the warm water in a pitcher, stir in the sugar and yeast, and let stand for 15 minutes.

2 Mix the flours, salt, nuts, and dried and fresh apple together in a large bowl. Make a well in the center, pour in the yeast mixture, and gradually work into the flour mixture. Mix in the remaining warm water and bring together to form a soft dough.

3 Turn out onto a floured counter and knead briefly. Shape the dough into a rectangle and place in the prepared pan. Cover with a warm, damp cloth and set aside in a warm place for 40 minutes, until the dough has risen.

4 Meanwhile, preheat the oven to 400°F/200°C. Remove the cloth and bake the loaf in the preheated oven for 40 minutes. Carefully lift out of the pan and return the loaf to the oven, upside down, for 10–15 minutes—the loaf should sound hollow when tapped on the bottom.

5 Remove from the oven and let cool on a wire rack. Slice and serve spread with honey, and sliced banana or nut butter. Store wrapped in foil for up to three days, or freeze for up to a month.

Baked Egg with Ham & Tomato

INGREDIENTS

1 tsp olive oil

½ small leek, chopped

2 slices wafer-thin ham, chopped

1 egg

¼ cup grated cheddar cheese

2 slices tomato

serves ❶

1 Preheat the oven to 350°F/180°C. Heat the oil in a pan and cook the leek for 5–6 minutes, until soft.

2 Place the leek in the bottom of a ramekin and top with the ham. Crack and pour in the egg, then top with the cheese and tomato.

3 Bake in the preheated oven for 10 minutes, until the egg is set. Remove the ramekin from the oven, let cool a little, wrap in a cloth, and serve.

Waffles with Caramelized Bananas

INGREDIENTS

1¼ cups all-purpose flour

2 tsp baking powder

½ tsp salt

2 tsp superfine sugar

2 eggs, separated

generous 1 cup milk

6 tbsp butter, melted

CARAMELIZED BANANAS

7 tbsp butter, cut into pieces

3 tbsp dark corn syrup

3 large ripe bananas, peeled
and thickly sliced

makes ❶❷ waffles

1 Mix the flour, baking powder, salt, and sugar together in a bowl. Whisk the egg yolks, milk, and melted butter together with a fork, then stir this mixture into the dry ingredients to make a smooth batter.

2 Using an electric mixer or hand whisk, whisk the egg whites in a clean bowl until stiff peaks form. Fold into the batter mixture. Spoon 2 large tablespoons of the batter into a preheated waffle maker and cook according to the manufacturer's instructions.

3 To make the caramelized bananas, melt the butter with the dark corn syrup in a saucepan over low heat and stir until combined. Let simmer for a few minutes until the caramel thickens and darkens slightly. Add the bananas and mix gently to coat. Pour over the warm waffles and serve immediately.

Fruity Maple Porridge

INGREDIENTS

serves ❶

¾ **cup whole milk or soy milk, plus extra for serving (optional)**

½ **cup oatmeal**

1 tbsp maple syrup or honey

mixed fresh fruit, such as apples, pears, bananas, peaches, mangoes, strawberries, and raspberries, prepared and chopped

1 Mix the milk and oatmeal together in a pan and cook over medium heat, stirring, for 8–10 minutes.

2 Serve drizzled with the maple syrup and topped with the fresh fruit, with a little more milk if needed.

2 Meat & Poultry

The recipes in this chapter can be enjoyed by adults and children alike. Pasta with meat sauce or tasty mini meatballs is a universal favorite, as are meat pie with a creamy potato topping, and finger-licking sticky drumsticks. There are exciting ideas from around the world, too. Older children will love the tasty flavors of sweet and sour chicken, fragrant Moroccan couscous, or mildly spicy Mexican-style wraps and quesadillas.

Mini Meatballs & Spaghetti

INGREDIENTS

makes ❽ to ❿ meatballs

2 oz/55 g lean ground beef

1 tsp finely chopped onion

2 tsp chopped fresh basil

1 tbsp freshly prepared whole wheat breadcrumbs

1 tsp olive oil

1½-2 cups tomato sauce

2 oz/55 g dried spaghetti, broken into short lengths

finely chopped fresh parsley (optional)

1 To make the meatballs, put the ground beef, onion, basil, and breadcrumbs into a small bowl and process using a hand blender. Divide and shape the mixture into even bite-size balls.

2 Heat the oil in a small saucepan and fry the meatballs, turning frequently, for 2–3 minutes, until lightly browned. Pour over the sauce, cover, and simmer gently for about 10 minutes.

3 Cook the spaghetti in a separate saucepan, according to the package instructions. Drain. Serve the spaghetti topped with the meatballs and sauce. Sprinkle with parsley, if liked.

Spaghetti Bolognese

INGREDIENTS

serves 4

12 oz/350 g spaghetti or pasta of your choice

BOLOGNESE SAUCE

2 tbsp olive oil

1 onion, finely chopped

2 garlic cloves, finely chopped

1 carrot, peeled and finely chopped

1½ cups mushrooms, peeled and sliced or chopped (optional)

1 tsp dried oregano

½ tsp dried thyme

1 bay leaf

10 oz/280 g lean ground beef

1¼ cups stock

1¼ cups strained tomatoes

pepper

grated Parmesan cheese, for sprinkling (optional)

1 To make the sauce, heat the oil in a heavy-bottom skillet. Add the onion and sauté, half covered, for 5 minutes, or until softened. Add the garlic, carrot, and mushrooms, if using, and sauté for another 3 minutes, stirring occasionally.

2 Add the herbs and ground beef to the pan and cook until the meat has browned, stirring regularly.

3 Add the stock and strained tomatoes. Reduce the heat, season to taste, and cook over a medium–low heat, half covered, for 15–20 minutes, or until the sauce has reduced and thickened. Remove the bay leaf.

4 Meanwhile, cook the pasta according to the instructions on the package, until the pasta is tender. Drain well and mix together the pasta and sauce until the pasta is well coated. Serve immediately, sprinkled with the grated Parmesan cheese, if liked.

Brilliant Hamburgers

INGREDIENTS

makes ❹ to ❻

1 lb/450 g ground beef

1 onion, finely chopped

1 egg, beaten

1 tbsp flour for shaping

1 tbsp olive oil

salt and pepper

TO SERVE

4–6 burger buns

half a lettuce

2 tomatoes

**mustard, ketchup,
or mayonnaise**

1 Put the ground beef in the mixing bowl and add the onion, egg, and seasoning. Mix well.

2 Lightly flour your hands and the cutting board. Divide the mixture into 4–6 equal portions and shape into hamburgers.

3 Chill the hamburgers in the refrigerator for 10 minutes. Preheat the broiler. Place the chilled hamburgers on the broiler pan and brush with oil.

4 Broil the hamburgers for 4–6 minutes. Turn them over, brush again with oil. Broil for another 4–6 minutes, until done.

5 Cut the buns in half. Toast them under the hot broiler if you wish. Slice the tomatoes thinly. Wash and shred the lettuce.

6 Place a handful of lettuce in each bun, then add the hamburger and a slice of tomato. Serve with your own choice of condiment.

Shepherd's Pie

INGREDIENTS

serves 4

2 tbsp olive oil

1 lb 10 oz/750 g lean fresh ground lamb or beef

1 leek, chopped

1 small red onion, chopped

2 carrots, chopped

1 celery stalk, chopped

3½ oz/100 g mushrooms, chopped

14 oz/400 g canned tomatoes

2 tbsp fresh thyme leaves

½ cup water

1 lb 2 oz/500 g potatoes, boiled and mashed

14 oz/400 g sweet potatoes, boiled and mashed

4 tbsp whole milk

piece of unsalted butter

salt and pepper

1 Heat half the oil in a nonstick skillet and cook the ground lamb over high heat, breaking up with a wooden spoon, until well browned. Remove the ground lamb from the skillet with a slotted spoon, pour away any fat, and wipe the skillet with paper towels.

2 Add the remaining oil to the skillet and cook the leek, onion, carrots, and celery for 15 minutes, until soft. Return the lamb to the pan and add the mushrooms, tomatoes, thyme, and water. Season to taste with salt and pepper and let simmer for 40 minutes, stirring occasionally.

3 Meanwhile, preheat the oven to 350°F/180°C. Mix the 2 mashes of potatoes with half the milk and half the butter in a bowl and season to taste with salt and pepper.

4 Spoon the meat sauce into a baking dish and top with the potato mixture. Brush with the remaining milk and dot with the remaining butter. Bake in the preheated oven for 35 minutes, until the topping is brown and crisp.

Ham Pizza

PIZZA DOUGH

heaping 1½ cups white bread flour

½ tsp salt

2 tsp easy-blend yeast

1 tbsp vegetable oil

¾ cup warm water

2 tbsp flour for dusting

TOPPING

14 oz/400 g canned chopped tomatoes

2 tbsp tomato paste

2 tsp dried oregano

2 slices of ham, torn into bite-size pieces

5½ oz/150 g mozzarella, torn into bite-size pieces

1 yellow bell pepper, sliced

4 button mushrooms, sliced

2 tbsp olive oil

salt and pepper

serves ❹

1 Mix the flour, salt, and yeast in a bowl then add the oil and water. Stir to form a soft dough. Knead the dough on a lightly floured surface until smooth and elastic. Place back in the bowl, cover, and leave in a warm place for an hour.

2 Once the dough has risen, flour your hands and the work surface. Knead the dough until smooth, stretch it into shape and roll thinly into two circles, each about 6 inches/15 cm across.

3 Pinch up the edges of the dough. Grease the baking sheets. Place the dough circles on the sheets and let them rise while you make the topping.

4 Preheat the oven to 425°F/220°C. Drain the tomatoes and put into a bowl with the paste and oregano. Mix and season.

5 Spread half the mixture over each dough circle. Arrange the ham, cheese, bell pepper, and mushrooms on top. Brush over the olive oil.

6 Bake in the oven for 15–20 minutes, until the crusts are pale golden and firm. Remove from the oven and serve.

Perfect Pasta

INGREDIENTS

serves 4

¼ tsp salt

9 oz/250 g pasta shapes

4 tbsp butter

heaping ¼ cup all-purpose flour

scant 2 cups milk

heaping 1 cup grated cheddar cheese

4½ oz/125 g cooked ham, roughly chopped

4 cherry tomatoes, cut into quarters

2 tbsp grated **Parmesan** cheese

1 Preheat the oven to 400°F/200°C. Heat some water in the large saucepan. Add salt and bring to a boil.

2 Add the pasta carefully, being careful not to splash. Cook the pasta according to the package instructions.

3 Gently melt the butter in a saucepan over a low heat. Add the flour and mix well. Cook the mixture for 1 minute, then remove from heat.

4 Stir in the milk, a little at a time, to make a smooth sauce. Put pan back on heat. Stir while the sauce thickens so it doesn't go lumpy.

5 When the sauce boils, turn down heat and cook, stirring, for 1–2 minutes. Remove from the heat. Mix in the cheddar, ham, and tomatoes. Season.

6 Drain the pasta. Mix with the sauce. Place in an ovenproof dish and sprinkle with Parmesan. Bake in oven, on a baking sheet, for 20–25 minutes.

Homemade Chicken Nuggets

INGREDIENTS

serves ❹

3 skinless, boneless chicken breasts

4 tbsp whole wheat all-purpose flour

1 tbsp wheat germ

½ tsp ground cumin

½ tsp ground coriander

1 egg, lightly beaten

2 tbsp olive oil

pepper

green salad, to serve

DIPPING SAUCE

3½ oz/100 g sunblush tomatoes

3½ oz/100 g fresh tomatoes, peeled, seeded, and chopped

2 tbsp mayonnaise

1 Preheat the oven to 375°F/190°C. Cut the chicken breasts into 1½-inch/4-cm chunks. Mix the flour, wheat germ, cumin, coriander, and pepper to taste in a bowl, then divide in half and put on 2 separate plates. Put the beaten egg on a third plate.

2 Pour the oil into a baking sheet with a rim and heat in the oven. Roll the chicken pieces in one plate of flour, shake to remove any excess, then roll in the egg and in the second plate of flour, again shaking off any excess flour. When all the nuggets are ready, remove the baking sheet from the oven and toss the nuggets in the hot oil. Roast in the oven for 25–30 minutes, until golden and crisp.

3 Meanwhile, to make the dipping sauce, put both kinds of tomatoes in a blender or food processor and process until smooth. Add the mayonnaise and process again until well combined.

4 Remove the nuggets from the oven and drain on paper towels. Serve with the dipping sauce and a green salad.

Chicken & Apple Bites

INGREDIENTS

1 apple, peeled, cored, and grated

2 skinless, boneless chicken breasts, cut into chunks

½ red onion, minced

1 tbsp minced fresh parsley

scant 1 cup fresh whole wheat breadcrumbs

1 tbsp concentrated chicken stock

whole wheat flour, for coating

peanut oil, for pan-frying

makes ❷❹

1 Spread the apple out on a clean dish towel and press out all the excess moisture.

2 Put the chicken, apple, onion, parsley, breadcrumbs, and stock in a food processor or blender and blend briefly until well combined.

3 Spread the flour out on a plate. Divide the mixture into 24 mini portions, shape each portion into a ball, and roll in the flour.

4 Heat a little oil in a nonstick skillet over medium heat and cook the balls for 5–8 minutes, or until golden brown all over and cooked through. Remove and drain on paper towels. Serve hot, or cold for a lunchbox.

Chicken Satay Bites

INGREDIENTS

serves 4

4 skinless, boneless chicken breasts, about 5 oz/140 g each

2 tbsp extra virgin olive oil

2 tbsp lemon juice

SATAY SAUCE

4½ oz/125 g smooth no-sugar peanut butter

1½ tbsp olive oil

2 tbsp hot water

1½ tbsp light soy sauce

2 tbsp fresh apple juice

4 tbsp coconut milk

1 To make the sauce, mix all the ingredients together in a serving bowl.

2 Soak 16 wooden skewers in water for at least 30 minutes to prevent them from burning. Cut each chicken breast lengthwise into 4 strips and thread each strip onto a skewer.

3 Mix the oil and lemon juice together in a small bowl, then brush over the chicken.

4 Preheat a griddle pan or broiler to medium-high. Cook the chicken skewers, in batches, for 3 minutes on each side, or until golden and cooked through, making sure that there is no trace of pink inside. Keep the cooked chicken skewers warm while cooking the remaining skewers. Serve the skewers with the sauce.

Sweet & Sour Chicken Stir-Fry

INGREDIENTS

2 oz/55 g medium egg noodles

1 tbsp vegetable oil

2 oz/55 g skinless, boneless chicken breast, cut into thin strips

½ small carrot, cut into matchsticks

2 baby corn, halved widthwise and lengthwise

4 sugar snap peas, cut into strips

2 oz/55 g pineapple, chopped

2 scallions, sliced

1 oz/25 g bok choy or baby spinach, roughly torn

1 tsp pineapple juice

1 tsp light soy sauce

1 tsp rice or sherry vinegar

TO SERVE

soy sauce (optional)

sweet chili sauce (optional)

serves ❷

1 Cook or soak the noodles according to the package instructions. Heat the oil in a wok and stir-fry the chicken until lightly browned and cooked through. Add the carrot, baby corn, sugar snap peas, pineapple, and scallions and cook for 1–2 minutes. Add the bok choy, pineapple juice, soy sauce, and vinegar, and stir together until the bok choy has just wilted.

2 Drain the noodles and serve topped with the chicken and vegetables. Add a little more soy sauce if liked; older children may like a little sweet chili sauce with this.

Chicken Quesadilla Triangles

INGREDIENTS

serves ❶ to ❷

2 small (8-inch/20-cm) flour tortillas

1–2 tsp melted butter, for brushing

½ small cooked skinless, boneless chicken breast, finely chopped

¾ cup grated cheddar (or a mixture of cheddar and mozzarella cheese)

1 tomato, skinned, seeded, and diced

2 tsp sour cream seasoned with a squeeze of lime juice and a little chopped cilantro

1 Preheat the oven to 400°F/200°C.

2 Lightly brush one tortilla with a little melted butter and place, butter-side down, on a baking sheet. Arrange the chicken, cheese, and tomato over the tortilla, leaving a gap around the edge.

3 Place the second tortilla on top and brush with the remaining butter. Bake for about 10 minutes, until the cheese has melted and the top is brown. Let cool slightly, then cut into triangles and serve with sour cream.

Tex-Mex Roll Ups

INGREDIENTS

serves ❷

2 corn tortillas

**2 tbsp Boston Baked Beans
or canned organic baked
beans, mashed**

**2 tbsp grated cheddar
cheese**

**2–3 tbsp cooked chicken,
finely chopped or shredded**

1 tomato, sliced

**¼ avocado, peeled and cut
into strips**

1 Put each tortilla on a microwavable plate.
Spread the beans over each tortilla and
sprinkle with the cheese. Microwave for about
15 seconds, until the cheese melts. Cool
slightly. Arrange the chicken, tomato, and
avocado on top. Roll up and cut into small
pieces.

Sticky Drumsticks & Cucumber Salad

INGREDIENTS

serves 6

6 chicken drumsticks

2 tbsp maple syrup

2 tbsp low-salt soy sauce

1 tsp sesame oil

½ cucumber, thinly sliced

2 scallions, thinly sliced

salt

1 Preheat the oven to 375°F/190°C. Trim the chicken drumsticks of any excess skin and pat dry with paper towels.

2 Mix the maple syrup, soy sauce, and sesame oil in a large bowl. Add the chicken drumsticks and toss well to coat.

3 Place the chicken drumsticks on a nonstick baking sheet and roast in the preheated oven for 30–40 minutes, basting occasionally, until the chicken is tender, well browned, and sticky, and the juices run clear when a skewer is inserted into the thickest part of the meat.

4 Meanwhile, put the cucumber in a colander and sprinkle with a little salt. Let stand for 10 minutes until the juices have drained out. Pat dry with paper towels and mix with the scallions.

5 Serve the chicken hot or cold with the cucumber salad.

3 Fish & Seafood

It often seems an easy option to choose packaged fish sticks or fish cakes, but what could be more satisfying than preparing your own? Children love them made with flavorsome fish, such as salmon or tuna. Pasta mixed with tiny nuggets of fish is easy to eat and never fails to please—even the fussiest eater will be clamoring for seconds. Fish and rice is another foolproof option—mixed with eggs it is particularly delicious and healthy, too.

Tuna & Pasta Salad

INGREDIENTS

serves ❷

3½ oz/100 g small
whole wheat pasta

2 tbsp olive oil

1 tbsp mayonnaise

1 tbsp plain yogurt

2 tbsp pesto

7 oz/200 g canned tuna in
spring water, drained and
flaked

7 oz/200 g canned no-added-
sugar corn kernels, drained

2 tomatoes, peeled, seeded,
and chopped

½ green bell pepper, seeded
and chopped

½ avocado, pitted, peeled,
and chopped

salt and pepper

1 Cook the pasta in a large pan of boiling water for 8–10 minutes, until only just tender. Drain, return to the pan, and add half the oil. Toss well to coat, then cover and let cool.

2 Whisk the mayonnaise, yogurt, and pesto together in a pitcher, adding a little oil if needed to achieve the desired consistency. Add a pinch of salt and season to taste with pepper.

3 Mix the cooled pasta with the tuna, corn, tomatoes, green bell pepper, and avocado, add the dressing, and toss well to coat.

Tortillas with Tuna, Egg, & Corn

INGREDIENTS

1 tbsp plain yogurt

1 tsp olive oil

½ tsp white wine vinegar

½ tsp Dijon mustard

1 large egg, hard-cooked and cooled

7 oz/200 g canned tuna in spring water, drained

7 oz/200 g canned no-added-sugar corn kernels, drained

2 whole wheat flour tortillas

1 container fine curled cress or alfalfa sprouts

pepper

serves ❷

1 To make the dressing, whisk the yogurt, oil, vinegar, and mustard, and pepper to taste in a pitcher until emulsified and smooth.

2 Shell the egg, separate the yolk and the white, then mash the yolk and mince the white. Mash the tuna with the egg and dressing, then mix in the corn.

3 Spread the filling equally over the 2 tortillas and sprinkle over the cress. Fold in one end and roll up. Wrap in foil for a packed lunch.

Tuna Bites

INGREDIENTS

serves 4

7 oz/200 g canned tuna in spring water, drained

1 egg

1 tsp minced fresh parsley

scant 1 cup fresh whole wheat breadcrumbs

about 1 tbsp whole wheat all-purpose flour

vegetable oil, for brushing

salt and pepper

1 Mash the tuna with the egg, parsley, and a pinch of salt and pepper to taste. Add the breadcrumbs and mix well, then add enough of the flour to bind the mixture together.

2 Divide the mixture into 20 mini portions, shape each portion into a ball, and let chill for 15 minutes.

3 Meanwhile, preheat the oven to 375°F/190°C. Brush a nonstick baking sheet with a little oil. Space the tuna balls out on the baking sheet and brush with a little more oil. Bake in the preheated oven for 15–20 minutes, until golden and crisp.

4 Remove from the oven and drain on paper towels. Serve warm or cold.

Homemade Fish Sticks & Sweet Potato Wedges

INGREDIENTS

10 oz/280 g thick cod fillets, skin and bones removed

flour, for dusting

1 tsp paprika

fresh breadcrumbs or fine cornmeal, for coating

1 egg, beaten

sunflower oil, for frying

fresh peas or frozen peas, cooked, to serve

SWEET POTATO WEDGES

1 lb/450 g sweet potatoes, scrubbed and cut into wedges

1 tbsp olive oil

salt and pepper

makes 8 to 10

1 To make the potato wedges, preheat the oven to 400°F/200°C.

2 Dry the sweet potato wedges on a clean dish towel. Place the oil in a roasting pan and heat for a few minutes in the oven. Arrange the potatoes in the pan and bake for 30–35 minutes, turning them halfway through, until tender and golden.

3 Meanwhile, cut the cod into strips about ¾-inch/2-cm wide.

4 Put the flour onto a plate, add the paprika, and season to taste. Put the breadcrumbs onto a second plate. Roll the cod strips in the seasoned flour until coated, shaking off any excess, then dip them in the beaten egg. Roll the cod strips in the breadcrumbs until evenly coated.

5 Heat enough oil to cover the bottom of a large, nonstick skillet. Carefully arrange the fish sticks in the pan—you may have to cook them in batches—and fry them for 3–4 minutes on each side, or until crisp and golden. Drain on paper towels before serving, if necessary.

6 Serve the fish sticks with the sweet potato wedges and peas.

Two-Fish Casserole

INGREDIENTS

makes ❹ to ❻

3 oz/85 g penne or macaroni

2 tsp olive oil, plus extra for coating pasta

1 egg

1 small onion, finely chopped

1 small celery stalk, finely chopped

1 small carrot, peeled and finely chopped

small handful of spinach leaves, tough stalks removed and finely shredded

½ cup milk

2 tbsp heavy cream

¼ cup mature cheddar cheese

½ tsp English mustard

3¼ oz/90 g undyed smoked haddock, skinned and boned

5 oz/140 g white fish, skinned and boned

3 oz/85 g mozzarella cheese, diced

1 Preheat the oven to 400°F/200°C. Cook the pasta according to the instructions on the package until tender. Drain well. Toss in oil.

2 Bring a small saucepan of water to a boil and add the egg. Cook for 8–10 minutes, until the egg is hard boiled. Cool the egg under cold running water.

3 Heat the oil in a heavy-bottom skillet. Add the onion and sauté for 5 minutes, until softened, then add the celery and carrot and sauté for 3 minutes. Add the spinach and cook for another 2 minutes, until tender.

4 Stir in the milk and cream and bring to the boil. Turn off the heat and stir in the cheddar cheese and mustard.

5 Place the fish in a small ovenproof dish. Shell and chop the hard-boiled egg and spoon it over the fish, then top with the sauce. Arrange the pasta over the top and sprinkle with the mozzarella cheese. Bake for 20–25 minutes, until browned on top.

Salmon Cakes

INGREDIENTS

makes **❶❷**

1 lb 9 oz/700 g skinless salmon fillet, cut into cubes

1¼ cups whole milk

1 bay leaf

3½ oz/100 g broccoli, steamed until tender

1 lb 9 oz/700 g potatoes, boiled and mashed

2 tbsp minced fresh parsley

4 tbsp whole wheat all-purpose flour

1 egg yolk

2 large eggs, beaten

2¾ cups fresh whole wheat breadcrumbs

2 tbsp olive oil

pepper

1 Preheat the oven to 400°F/200°C. Put the salmon in a pan with the milk and bay leaf and bring slowly to simmering point. Let simmer for 2 minutes, then remove the pan from the heat, lift out and discard the bay leaf, and let the fish stand in the milk to cool. When cool, lift out the fish with a slotted spoon onto paper towels to drain.

2 Flake the fish into a large bowl. Put the broccoli in a food processor and blend until smooth. Add to the fish with the mashed potatoes, parsley, 1 tablespoon of the flour, and pepper to taste. Add the egg yolk and mix well. If the mixture is a little dry, add some of the poaching milk; if too wet, add a little more flour.

3 Divide the mixture into 12 portions and shape each portion into a cake. Put the beaten eggs, remaining flour, and the breadcrumbs on 3 separate plates. Roll each fish cake in the flour, then in the beaten egg, and then in the breadcrumbs to coat.

4 Heat the oil in a nonstick baking sheet with a rim in the preheated oven for 5 minutes. Add the fish cake and bake for 10 minutes, then carefully turn the fish cake over and bake for an additional 10 minutes.

Salmon with Egg-Fried Rice

INGREDIENTS

serves 2

7 oz/200 g skinless salmon fillet

2 tsp clear honey

1 tbsp light soy sauce

3 tsp vegetable oil

1 small carrot, finely chopped

2 tbsp frozen peas

½ red bell pepper, seeded and chopped

1 egg, beaten

3 oz/85 g basmati rice, cooked

1 scallion, finely sliced

lightly cooked spinach or bok choy, to serve

1 Cut the salmon into 2 pieces and place in a shallow dish. Mix together the honey and soy sauce and brush over the salmon. Let stand for 10 minutes.

2 Heat 2 teaspoons of the oil and cook the carrot for about 5 minutes. Add the peas and bell pepper and cook for another 5 minutes until softened. Add the beaten egg and cook over gentle heat, stirring and breaking up the egg into little pieces. Add the cooked rice and heat through for a few minutes.

3 Heat the remaining oil in a small skillet and cook the salmon for 2–3 minutes on each side. Alternatively, cook the fish under the broiler. Stir the scallion into the rice. Serve the salmon on a bed of spinach and accompanied with the egg-fried rice.

Creamy Smoked Salmon & Broccoli Pasta

INGREDIENTS

serves 4

14 oz/400 g pasta shells, bows, or tagliatelle

8 oz/225 g broccoli florets

1 tbsp olive oil

2 tbsp butter

1 leek, finely chopped

7 oz/200 g tub garlic and herb soft cheese

6 tbsp whole milk

3½ oz/100 g smoked salmon pieces

salt and pepper

1 Cook the pasta according to the instructions on the package, until the pasta is tender, then drain. Meanwhile, steam the broccoli for 8–10 minutes, or until tender.

2 At the same time, prepare the sauce. Heat the oil and butter in a small heavy-bottom skillet, then add the leek and sauté for 7 minutes, or until softened. Gently stir in the soft cheese and milk and heat through.

3 Add the smoked salmon pieces and cook for a minute or so, until they turn opaque. Combine the sauce with the pasta and broccoli and mix together well. Season.

Honey Salmon Kebabs

INGREDIENTS

serves ❷

4 boneless salmon fillets, each about 5 oz/140 g, skinned and cut into ¾-inch/2-cm cubes

1 tbsp toasted sesame seeds (optional)

MARINADE

2 tbsp clear honey

1 tbsp soy sauce

1 tbsp olive oil

1 tsp toasted sesame oil

1 Mix together the ingredients for the marinade in a shallow dish. Add the salmon and stir to coat the fish in the marinade. Let marinate in the refrigerator for 1 hour, turning the fish occasionally.

2 Preheat the broiler to high. Thread the cubes of salmon onto 4–6 skewers. Line a broiler rack with foil and place the skewers on top. Brush the salmon with the marinade and broil for 3–5 minutes, turning the skewers occasionally, until cooked.

3 While the salmon is cooking, put the remaining marinade in a small saucepan and heat for a few minutes, until it has reduced and thickened.

4 Serve the kebabs with rice. Spoon the reduced marinade over the salmon and sprinkle with sesame seeds, if using.

Fish Pie

INGREDIENTS

serves ❹

1 tbsp olive oil

1 onion, finely chopped

1 celery stalk, finely chopped

1 carrot, peeled and finely chopped

small handful of spinach leaves, tough stalks removed and finely shredded

1 cup milk

4 tbsp heavy cream

½ cup grated mature cheddar cheese

1 tsp Dijon mustard

2 tbsp finely chopped fresh parsley

squeeze of fresh lemon juice

8 oz/225 g undyed smoked haddock, skin and bones removed, cut into pieces

8 oz/225 g cod fillet, skin and bones removed

2 hard-boiled eggs

1 sheet of prepared puff pastry, defrosted if using frozen

1 egg, beaten, to glaze

salt and pepper

1 Preheat the oven to 400°F/200°C.

2 Heat the oil in a heavy-bottom skillet. Add the onion and sauté for 5 minutes, or until softened, then add the celery and carrot and sauté for 3 minutes. Add the spinach and cook for another 2 minutes, or until tender.

3 Stir in the milk and cream and bring to a boil. Turn off the heat and stir in the cheddar cheese, mustard, parsley, and lemon juice. Season to taste.

4 Place the fish in an ovenproof dish. Peel and chop the egg and spoon it over the fish, then top with the creamy vegetable sauce.

5 Place the pastry on a lightly floured counter. Make fish and starfish shapes, using cookie cutters, then arrange them on top of the fish pie. Brush the pastry shapes with beaten egg and bake for 20–25 minutes, or until the fish is cooked and the pastry shapes have risen and are a golden brown color.

Sunny Rice

INGREDIENTS

serves 4

1 lb/450 g undyed smoked haddock or cod fillets

milk or water, for poaching the fish

2 cups water

1 cup basmati rice, rinsed

1 bay leaf

2 cloves

4 tbsp butter

½ cup frozen petit pois

1 tsp garam masala

½ tsp ground turmeric

2 tbsp chopped flat-leaf parsley

4 hard-boiled eggs, quartered

pepper

1 Put the haddock in a large skillet and pour enough milk or water over the fish to just cover it. Poach the fish for 5 minutes, or until cooked and opaque. Remove the haddock from the pan and flake the fish, carefully removing the skin and any bones. Discard the remainder of the poaching liquid.

2 Meanwhile, place the rice in a saucepan and cover with the measured water, then add the bay leaf and cloves. Bring to a boil, then reduce the heat and simmer, covered, for 15 minutes, or until the water has been absorbed and the rice is tender. Discard the bay leaf and cloves. Set aside the covered pan.

3 Melt the butter over gentle heat in the cleaned skillet, then add the peas and cook for 2 minutes, or until tender. Stir in the garam masala and turmeric and cook for another minute.

4 Stir in the haddock and rice and mix well until they are coated in the spiced butter.

5 Season and heat through for 1–2 minutes. Stir in the parsley and top with the hard-boiled eggs just before serving.

Surf 'n' Turf Paella

INGREDIENTS

serves ❷ to ❸

2 tbsp olive oil

1 onion, diced

2 skinless chicken breasts, sliced

1 small red bell pepper, seeded and diced

2 garlic cloves, chopped

1 tomato, seeded and chopped

1 tbsp tomato paste

pinch of saffron

2½ cups hot chicken or vegetable stock

scant 1 cup paella rice

½ cup frozen peas

4 oz/115 g cooked shrimp, defrosted if frozen

salt and pepper

1 Heat the oil in a large heavy-bottom sauté pan (with a lid). Add the onion and fry for 5 minutes, or until softened. Add the chicken breast, bell pepper, and garlic and sauté for 5 minutes over medium heat, stirring frequently to prevent the mixture from sticking.

2 Add the tomato, tomato paste, saffron, and stock to the pan. Stir in the rice and bring to a boil, then reduce the heat. Simmer the rice, covered, for 15 minutes, or until the rice is tender.

3 Add the peas, shrimp, and seasoning and cook for another 2–3 minutes, or until the shrimp have heated through.

Shrimp with Coconut Rice

INGREDIENTS

serves ❹

1 cup dried Chinese mushrooms

2 tbsp vegetable or peanut oil

6 scallions, chopped

scant ½ cup dry unsweetened coconut

1 fresh green chile, seeded and chopped

heaping 1 cup jasmine rice

⅔ cup fish stock

1¾ cups coconut milk

12 oz/350 g cooked shelled shrimp

6 sprigs fresh Thai basil

1 Place the mushrooms in a small bowl, cover with hot water, and set aside to soak for 30 minutes. Drain, then cut off and discard the stalks and slice the caps.

2 Heat the oil in a wok and stir-fry the scallions, coconut, and chile for 2–3 minutes, until lightly browned. Add the mushrooms and stir-fry for 3–4 minutes.

3 Add the rice and stir-fry for 2–3 minutes, then add the stock and bring to a boil. Reduce the heat and add the coconut milk. Let simmer for 10–15 minutes, until the rice is tender. Stir in the shrimp and basil, heat through, and serve.

4 Vegetables

Vegetables are vital for health, but getting children to eat them can be a challenge. Try recipes using corn or carrots—young children love the bright colors. Chopped small or pureed, vegetables are easier to chew and swallow. They can be disguised in nutritious soups or served as part of a dish based on energy-rich foods, such as eggs, pasta, or beans. Vegetable-based omelets, lasagna, and bean burgers are a hit with children of all ages.

Minestrone Soup

INGREDIENTS

serves ❷ to ❹

1 tbsp sunflower oil

2 tbsp chopped onion

1 garlic clove, chopped

½ tsp Italian herb seasoning

1¼ cup chopped carrot

2 tsp very finely chopped celery

¼ cup peeled and chopped potato

1¼ cups unsalted vegetable or chicken stock

scant ½ cup strained tomatoes

1 tsp tomato paste

1 oz/25 g dried vermicelli, broken into small pieces

1 tbsp frozen petit pois

10 baby spinach leaves, washed

cheese straws, to serve

1 To make the soup, heat the oil in a small saucepan. Add the onion and cook for a few minutes, until softened but not browned. Add the garlic, seasoning, carrot, celery, and potato and cook for 1–2 minutes.

2 Stir in the stock, drained tomatoes, and tomato paste. Bring to a boil, add the pasta and peas and then simmer for about 10 minutes, until the vegetables are tender.

3 Stir in the spinach leaves, remove from the heat, and cool a little before serving with the cheese straws.

Herbed Vegetable & Pasta Cheese

INGREDIENTS

makes ❹ to ❻ portions

4 florets broccoli, cut into small florets

4 florets cauliflower, cut into small florets

3 oz/85 g small penne or farfalle pasta

CHEESE SAUCE

1½ tbsp unsalted butter or margarine

1 tbsp all-purpose flour

¾ cup milk

½ tsp dried oregano

½ cup grated cheddar cheese

1 Steam the broccoli and cauliflower for 8–10 minutes, until tender. Cook the pasta according to the instructions on the package, until the pasta is tender, then drain.

2 Meanwhile, make the cheese sauce. Melt the butter in a small heavy-bottom saucepan over low heat. Gradually add the flour, beating well to form a smooth paste. Cook for 30 seconds, stirring continuously. Add the milk, a little at a time, whisking well to prevent any lumps from forming, then stir in the oregano. Simmer for 2 minutes, until smooth and creamy, then mix in the cheese. Stir until melted.

3 Add the cooked vegetables and pasta to the sauce and stir well. Finely chop or mash the mixture.

Chinese Noodles

INGREDIENTS

serves 4

9 oz/250 g package of tofu, drained and cubed

9 oz/250 g medium egg noodles

1 tbsp peanut or vegetable oil

1 red bell pepper, deseeded and sliced

8 oz/225 g broccoli florets

6 oz/175 g baby corn, halved lengthwise

2–3 tbsp water

2 scallions, finely sliced

1 tbsp sesame seeds, toasted (optional)

salt

MARINADE

1 garlic clove, finely chopped

1-inch/2.5-cm piece fresh ginger, peeled and grated

1 tsp sesame oil

1 tbsp clear honey

2 tbsp dark soy sauce

1 Mix together the ingredients for the marinade in a shallow dish. Add the tofu and spoon the marinade over. Refrigerate for 1 hour to marinate, turning the tofu occasionally to let the flavors steep.

2 Preheat the oven to 400°F/200°C. Using a slotted spoon, remove the tofu from the marinade and reserve the liquid. Arrange the tofu on a baking sheet and roast for 20 minutes, turning occasionally, until the tofu pieces are golden and crisp on all sides.

3 Meanwhile, cook the noodles in plenty of salted boiling water according to the instructions on the package, until the noodles are tender, then drain. Rinse the noodles under cold running water and drain again.

4 Heat a wok or heavy-bottom skillet, then add the oil. Add the bell pepper, broccoli, and corn and stir-fry, tossing and stirring continuously, over a medium-high heat for 5–8 minutes, or until the vegetables have softened. Add the water and continue to stir-fry until the vegetables are just tender but remain slightly crunchy.

5 Stir in the marinade, noodles, tofu, and scallions and stir-fry until heated through. Serve sprinkled with sesame seeds, if using.

Vegetable Lasagna

INGREDIENTS

1 tbsp olive oil

1 red onion, chopped

1 garlic clove, crushed and chopped

3½ oz/100 g zucchini, sliced

3½ oz/100 g baby spinach, washed and roughly torn

9 oz/250 g ricotta cheese

3–4 sheets fresh lasagna

1¾ cups tomato sauce or vegetable sauce

1¾ cups cheese sauce

3½ oz/100 g mozzarella cheese, roughly chopped

½ cup grated fresh Parmesan cheese

makes ❸ to ❹ invidual lasagna

1 Preheat the oven to 375°F/190°C.

2 Heat the oil in a saucepan, add the onion and garlic, and cook very slowly for about 10 minutes until soft. Add the zucchini and cook for 2–3 minutes. Add the spinach and stir until just wilted then remove from the heat. Let to cool then drain off any liquid.

3 Mix the cooked vegetables with the ricotta cheese. If necessary, blanch the lasagna according to the package instructions. Cut each lasagna sheet into pieces to fit individual ovenproof dishes about 5 inches/12 cm square. Spoon a little tomato sauce into each dish. Layer the lasagna, ricotta cheese mixture, and tomato sauce in each of the dishes. End with a layer of lasagna. Pour cheese sauce over each lasagna and sprinkle with the mozzarella and Parmesan cheeses.

4 Bake for about 20–25 minutes, until golden brown.

Hearty Bean & Pasta Soup

INGREDIENTS

serves ❹

4 tbsp olive oil

1 onion, finely chopped

1 celery stalk, chopped

1 carrot, peeled and diced

1 bay leaf

5 cups low-salt vegetable stock

14 oz/400 g can chopped tomatoes

6 oz/175 g pasta shapes, such as farfalle, shells, or twists

14 oz/400 g can cannellini beans, drained and rinsed

7 oz/200 g spinach or Swiss chard, thick stalks removed and shredded

⅓ cup finely grated Parmesan cheese

salt and pepper

1 Heat the olive oil in a large, heavy-bottom saucepan. Add the onion, celery, and carrot and cook over medium heat for 8–10 minutes, stirring occasionally, until the vegetables have softened.

2 Add the bay leaf, stock, and chopped tomatoes, then bring to a boil. Reduce the heat, cover, and simmer for 15 minutes, or until the vegetables are just tender.

3 Add the pasta and beans, then bring the soup back to a boil and cook for 10 minutes, or until the pasta is just tender. Stir occasionally to prevent the pasta from sticking to the bottom of the pan and burning.

4 Season to taste, add the spinach, and cook for another 2 minutes, or until tender. Serve, sprinkled with Parmesan cheese.

Creamy Tomato Soup

INGREDIENTS

serves ❹

1 tbsp butter

½ red onion, minced

1 leek, chopped

1 garlic clove, crushed

1 carrot, peeled and grated

1 potato, peeled and grated

1½ cups low-salt vegetable stock

1 lb 2 oz/500 g ripe tomatoes, peeled, seeded, and chopped

1 tbsp tomato paste

⅔ cup whole milk

salt and pepper

snipped chives, to garnish (optional)

whole wheat rolls, to serve

1 Melt the butter in a large pan over low heat and cook the onion, leek, and garlic for 10 minutes, or until very soft but not browned.

2 Add the carrot and potato and cook for 5 minutes.

3 Add the stock and bring to simmering point.

4 Add the tomatoes and tomato paste and season to taste with salt and pepper. Let simmer for 15 minutes, until the vegetables are very soft. Add the milk and warm through, then transfer the soup to a blender or food processor and process until very smooth. You can pass the soup through a strainer at this stage, if you like.

5 Return the soup to the rinsed-out pan and reheat gently. Garnish the soup with snipped chives, if desired, and serve with whole wheat rolls.

Warm Pasta Salad

INGREDIENTS

serves ❹

5 tbsp olive oil

1 tbsp lemon juice

2 garlic cloves, flattened with the back of a knife and chopped

1 tsp chopped fresh rosemary

2 tsp chopped fresh thyme

1 red onion, cut into 8 wedges

1 red bell pepper, seeded and thickly sliced

1 yellow pepper, seeded and thickly sliced

4 small zucchini, quartered lengthwise

4 plum tomatoes, quartered

9 oz/250 g penne pasta

1 tbsp white wine vinegar

1 tbsp pesto

7 oz/200 g feta cheese, crumbled

handful baby arugula leaves

1 Preheat the oven to 400°F/200°C.

2 Put 2 tablespoons of oil, the lemon juice, garlic, and herbs into a large baking pan. Add the onions and bell peppers and toss in the oil mixture. Cook in the oven for 10–15 minutes. Add the zucchini and tomatoes and cook for another 10–15 minutes, until the vegetables are soft and lightly charred on the edges.

3 Meanwhile, cook the pasta according to the package instructions. Drain and put into a large bowl. Mix together the remaining oil, vinegar, and pesto, and pour over the pasta. Add the cooled, cooked vegetables and the cheese and toss gently together. Sprinkle over the arugula and serve warm.

Chinese Rice with Omelet Strips

INGREDIENTS

serves ❷

2 tsp vegetable oil

few drops of sesame oil

1 small garlic clove, finely chopped

pinch of Chinese five spice

1 carrot, peeled and diced

2 baby corn, halved and thinly sliced

2 tbsp water

small handful of baby spinach, tough stems removed and finely sliced

1¼ cups cold, cooked brown or white rice

dash of soy sauce

1 tsp sesame seeds (optional)

small pat of unsalted butter

1 egg, beaten

1 Heat the vegetable oil and sesame oil in a wok or heavy-bottom skillet. Add the garlic, five spice, carrot, and baby corn and stir-fry for 5 minutes, stirring and tossing continuously to prevent the spices and vegetables from burning and sticking.

2 Add the water and stir-fry for 2 minutes, then mix in the spinach and cook, stirring frequently, for another 2 minutes, or until the vegetables are tender.

3 Add the rice and a dash of soy sauce to the wok or pan and heat through thoroughly. Mix in the sesame seeds, if using.

4 Meanwhile, melt the butter in a small heavy-bottom skillet and add the egg. Swirl the egg until it covers the bottom of the pan. Cook until the egg has set and is cooked through, then turn out onto a plate. Cut the omelette into strips or pieces.

5 Place the rice in a bowl and arrange the omelette in a crisscross pattern on top.

Cheesy Corn Fritters

INGREDIENTS

1 egg

scant 1 cup milk

¾ cup all-purpose flour

½ tsp baking powder

3 oz/85 g canned corn kernels without salt or sugar, drained

4 tbsp grated cheddar cheese

1 tsp snipped fresh chives

2 tsp sunflower oil, for frying

extra corn and mini carrot sticks, to serve

makes ❹ to ❻

1 Put the egg and milk into a small bowl and beat with a fork. Add the flour and baking powder and beat until smooth. Stir in the corn, cheese, and chives. Heat a little sunflower oil in a skillet and drop either teaspoonfuls or tablespoonfuls of the batter into it. Cook for 1–2 minutes on each side, until the fritters are puffed up and golden.

2 Drain on paper towels and serve with extra corn and mini carrot sticks.

Deep-Pan Omelet

INGREDIENTS

serves ❷ to ❹

1 tbsp sunflower oil

½ small onion, chopped

7 oz/200 g diced waxy potatoes

½ red bell pepper, seeded and thinly sliced

1 small zucchini, diced

1 tbsp chopped fresh parsley

2 tbsp frozen petit pois

3 eggs, beaten

1 Heat the oil in a 8-inch/20-cm omelet pan. Add the onion and cook for about 5 minutes, until softened. Add the potatoes and cook gently for about 10 minutes, until softened. Add the bell pepper, zucchini, petit pois, and parsley and cook for 2–3 minutes.

2 Beat the eggs with 1 tablespoon cold water. Pour over the vegetables in the skillet. Cook over very low heat for 5–10 minutes, or until the mixture is beginning to set on top and is golden underneath when the edge is lifted with a spatula.

3 Place under a medium broiler for 1–2 minutes, until the top is set and golden brown. Cool and then cut into wedges or strips to serve.

Roast Vegetable Lasagna

INGREDIENTS

serves ❹

3 tbsp olive oil

4 zucchini, halved lengthwise and thickly sliced

3 red bell peppers, seeded and chopped

1 eggplant, chopped

2 red onions, chopped

5 shallots, peeled and quartered

9 oz/250 g white mushrooms

14 oz/400 g canned chopped tomatoes

1 tbsp tomato paste

3½ tbsp butter

heaping ⅓ cup all-purpose flour or gluten-free flour

2½ cups milk

heaping ¾ cup grated cheddar cheese

7 oz/200 g fresh lasagna noodles

2 tbsp grated Parmesan cheese

salt and pepper

green salad, to serve

1 Preheat the oven to 375°F/190°C. Put the oil in a large bowl, add the zucchini, bell peppers, eggplant, onions, and shallots and toss well to coat.

2 Divide the vegetables between 2 baking sheets and roast in the preheated oven for 30–40 minutes, until soft and flecked with brown. Add the white mushrooms after 20 minutes.

3 Remove the vegetables from the oven and put into a large bowl. Add the tomatoes and tomato paste and mix well.

4 Melt the butter in a pan over low heat. Stir in the flour and cook, stirring constantly, for 2–3 minutes. Gradually add the milk and cook, continuing to stir constantly, until the sauce is thick and smooth. Season to taste with salt and pepper and stir in the cheddar cheese.

5 Layer the vegetable mixture and sauce in an ovenproof dish with the lasagna, finishing with a layer of sauce. Sprinkle over the Parmesan cheese and bake in the oven for 30–35 minutes.

6 Remove from the oven and serve hot with a green salad.

Bean Burgers

INGREDIENTS

14 oz/400 g canned cannellini beans, drained and rinsed

2 tbsp red pesto

1⅜ cups fresh whole wheat breadcrumbs

1 egg

2 tbsp olive oil

½ small red onion, minced

1 garlic clove, crushed

6 whole wheat rolls

6 tsp hummus

6 cherry tomatoes, sliced

sliced cucumber or cornichons

salt and pepper

salad greens, to serve

makes ❻

1 Mash the beans with a potato masher in a bowl until they are smooth, then add the pesto, breadcrumbs, egg, a pinch of salt, and pepper to taste, and mix well.

2 Heat half the oil in a nonstick skillet over low heat and cook the onion and garlic until softened. Add to the bean mixture and mix well.

3 Heat the remaining oil in the skillet. Spoon in the bean mixture, in 6 separate mounds, then press each one down with the back of a spoon to form a burger.

4 Cook the burgers for 4–5 minutes, then carefully turn over and cook for an additional 4–5 minutes, until golden.

5 Meanwhile, slice the rolls in half and smear each one with the hummus.

6 Remove the burgers from the skillet and drain on paper towels. Place each one in a roll, top with the tomatoes, cucumber, and salad greens, and serve.

Crispy Vegetable Bake

INGREDIENTS

2 tbsp butter, plus extra
for greasing

1 lb 10 oz/750 g potatoes,
thinly sliced

3 tbsp olive oil

1 garlic clove, crushed

1 tsp fresh oregano leaves

1 large leek, shredded

2 parsnips, peeled and
grated

3 carrots, peeled and grated

½ head celery root, peeled
and grated

7 oz/200 g feta cheese,
crumbled

4 eggs

salt and pepper

green salad, to serve

serves ❹

1 Preheat the oven to 375°F/190°C. Grease an 8-inch/20-cm round baking dish with butter.

2 Cook the potato slices in a large pan of boiling water for 5 minutes. Drain and cover with a clean dish towel to absorb the steam.

3 Melt half the butter with 1 tablespoon of the oil in a large skillet and cook the garlic, oregano, and leek for 3–4 minutes. Remove with a slotted spoon and transfer to a plate. Add the remaining oil to the skillet and cook the parsnips, carrots, and celery root for 10 minutes, until softened and cooked through. Season to taste with salt and pepper and cook for another 5 minutes. Stir in the leek mixture.

4 Arrange half the potato slices in the bottom of the prepared dish, top with half the vegetable mixture, and then sprinkle over half the cheese. Cover with the remaining vegetable mixture and cheese and top with the remaining potato slices. Dot with the remaining butter and bake in the preheated oven for 40 minutes, until golden and crisp.

5 Five minutes before serving, poach the eggs. Serve the vegetable bake topped with the poached eggs, accompanied by a green salad.

5 Snacks

Children's appetites are unpredictable but a tasty snack is always welcome, particularly after school when energy levels can be low. This chapter includes sweet and savory snacks to suit all appetites—from bite-size sandwiches for babies and toddlers, to hunky cheese on toast for ravenous school children. There are also recipes for healthy finger foods, such as dippers, nachos, and popcorn, that will be a real treat.

Simply Super Sandwich Fillings

INGREDIENTS

serves ④ to ⑥

TUNA & CORN

7 oz/200 g canned tuna in spring water, drained and flaked

1 tbsp canned corn, drained

1 tbsp chopped bell peppers

1 tbsp mayonnaise

FRUITY CHEESE SPREAD

3½ oz/100 g low-fat soft cheese or ricotta cheese

1 tbsp chopped, pitted dates

2 tbsp chopped, plumped dried apricots

CHICKEN & AVOCADO

½ cooked chicken breast, finely chopped

½ small avocado, mashed with 2 tsp lemon juice

1 Mix the ingredients for the fillings together and store in the refrigerator until required.

Hummus with Crunchy Vegetables

INGREDIENTS

makes ⓾ portions

7 oz/200 g no-salt, no-sugar canned chickpeas, drained and rinsed

½ garlic clove, crushed

3 tbsp tahini

freshly squeezed lemon juice, to taste

1 tbsp plain yogurt

carrot sticks, red bell pepper sticks, cucumber sticks, and apple wedges, to serve

1 Place the chickpeas in a blender with the garlic, tahini, lemon juice, and yogurt. Blend until smooth.

2 Store in the refrigerator for up to 3 days and serve with carrot sticks, red bell pepper sticks, cucumber sticks, and apple wedges.

Broiled Cheese Sandwich

INGREDIENTS

serves 4

1 stone-ground buckwheat boule loaf (about 7 inch/ 17.5 cm diameter) or other rustic round loaf

1½ cups finely shaved or coarsely grated cheddar cheese

1 large avocado, halved, pitted, peeled, and sliced

2 tomatoes, halved and cut into fine wedges

12 asparagus spears, cooked, bottled, or canned

4 slices Parma, Serrano, or Black Forest ham

olive oil

pepper

1 Slice the crusty top off the loaf; reserve for another use. Slice the loaf into two layers, making the bottom thicker. Place the bottom on a large piece of aluminum foil.

2 Preheat the broiler. Toast the top surface of the top layer of the loaf until brown, then turn it and place on the foil.

3 Sprinkle a heaping ¾ cup of cheese over both layers of bread. Arrange the avocado and tomato wedges on the bottom layer, then sprinkle with half the remaining cheese. Top with the asparagus spears and ham, completely covering the edges of the ingredients underneath. Sprinkle with the remaining cheese and a trickle of olive oil.

4 Cook well away from the heat source for 3–5 minutes. Remove the plain cheese-topped layer first, when the cheese is bubbling. Cook the bottom layer until the cheese has melted and the ham is browned.

5 Cut the toasted cheese layer into 8 wedges and overlap them on the filling, alternating the plain and cheese sides up. Serve at once, cut into 4 wedges.

Green Fingers

INGREDIENTS

2 soft tortillas

GUACAMOLE

½ avocado, pitted and flesh scooped out

½ garlic clove, crushed

squeeze of fresh lemon juice

makes ❷ portions

1 To make the guacamole, put the avocado, garlic, and lemon juice into a bowl. Mash with a fork until fairly smooth and creamy.

2 Warm the tortillas in a large dry skillet. Spread the guacamole over the tortillas and cut into fingers or wedges, or roll them up.

Cheese Twists

INGREDIENTS

serves ❹ to ❻

butter or margarine, for greasing

¾ cup Gruyère cheese, grated

½ tsp paprika

13 oz/375 g prepared puff pastry, defrosted if frozen

1 egg, beaten

1 Preheat the oven to 400°F/200°C. Grease a large baking sheet.

2 Mix together the Gruyère cheese and paprika and sprinkle over the sheet of puff pastry. Fold the puff pastry in half and roll out a little to seal the edges.

3 Cut the pastry into long ½-inch/1-cm wide strips, then cut each strip in half and gently twist. Place on the prepared baking sheet. Brush with the beaten egg and bake for 10–12 minutes, or until crisp and golden. Let cool on a wire rack.

Avocado Dip with Spicy Potato Skins

INGREDIENTS

serves **6** to **8**

4 large baking potatoes, scrubbed

3 tbsp olive oil

1 garlic clove, crushed

¼ tsp paprika

½ tsp dried red chile flakes (optional)

2 ripe avocados, pitted and peeled

juice of ½ lemon

5½ oz/150 g soft goat cheese

sea salt and pepper

1 Preheat the oven to 375°F/190°C. Rub the potatoes with 1 tablespoon of the oil, place on a baking sheet, and bake in the preheated oven for 1–1½ hours, until the flesh is soft.

2 Remove the potatoes from the oven, cut in half lengthwise, and carefully scoop out the flesh into a bowl, but leave a generous ½ inch/ 1 cm of the potato on the skins. Set aside the potato flesh for the dip.

3 Cut the skins into wedges. Put the remaining oil in a large bowl with the garlic, paprika, and chile flakes and mix until combined. Season sparingly with salt and pepper.

4 Toss the potato wedges in the spicy oil, spread out on the baking sheet, and bake in the oven for 20 minutes, until the skins are brown and crisp.

5 Meanwhile, to make the dip, in a separate bowl mash the avocado with the lemon juice, then mash in the cheese and potato flesh until well combined and smooth.

6 Serve the spicy skins warm, piled up, with little bowls of the dip.

Ham & Pineapple Muffin Pizzas

INGREDIENTS

makes ❽

4 English muffins

½ cup prepared tomato pizza sauce

2 sun-dried tomatoes in oil, chopped

2 oz/55 g Parma ham

2 rings canned pineapple, chopped

½ green bell pepper, seeded and chopped

4½ oz/125 g mozzarella cheese, cubed

olive oil, for drizzling

salt and pepper

fresh basil leaves, to garnish

1 Preheat the broiler to medium. Cut the English muffins in half and toast the cut side lightly under the broiler.

2 Spread the tomato sauce evenly over the English muffins. Sprinkle the sun-dried tomatoes on top of the tomato sauce.

3 Cut the Parma ham into thin strips and place on the English muffins with the pineapple and bell pepper. Carefully arrange the mozzarella cubes on top. Drizzle a little oil over each pizza and add salt and pepper to taste. Place under the hot broiler and cook until the cheese melts and bubbles. Serve at once, garnished with basil leaves.

Oven-Fried Chicken Wings

INGREDIENTS

serves ❹

12 chicken wings

1 egg

½ cup milk

heaping 4 tbsp all-purpose flour

1 tsp paprika

2 cups breadcrumbs

4 tbsp butter

salt and pepper

1 Preheat the oven to 425°F/220°C. Separate the chicken wings into 3 pieces each. Discard the bony tip. Beat the egg with the milk in a shallow dish. Combine the flour, paprika, and salt and pepper to taste in a separate shallow dish. Place the breadcrumbs in another shallow dish.

2 Dip the chicken pieces into the egg to coat well, then drain and roll in the seasoned flour. Remove, shaking off any excess, and roll the chicken in the breadcrumbs, gently pressing them onto the surface, then shaking off any excess.

3 Melt the butter in the preheated oven in a shallow roasting pan large enough to hold all the chicken pieces in a single layer. Arrange the chicken, skin-side down, in the pan and bake in the oven for 10 minutes. Turn and bake for an additional 10 minutes, or until the chicken is tender and the juices run clear when a skewer is inserted into the thickest part of the meat.

4 Remove the chicken from the pan and arrange on a large platter. Serve hot or at room temperature.

Nachos

INGREDIENTS

serves 6

6 oz/175 g tortilla chips

14 oz/400 g canned refried beans, warmed

2 tbsp finely chopped jarred jalapeño chiles

7 oz/200 g canned or jarred pimentos or roasted bell peppers, drained and finely sliced

1 cup grated Gruyère cheese

1 cup grated cheddar cheese

salt and pepper

1 Preheat the oven to 400°F/200°C.

2 Spread the tortilla chips out over the bottom of a large, shallow, ovenproof dish or roasting pan. Cover with the warmed refried beans. Sprinkle over the chiles and pimentos and season to taste with salt and pepper. Mix the cheeses together in a bowl and sprinkle on top.

3 Bake in the preheated oven for 5–8 minutes, or until the cheese is bubbling and melted. Serve at once.

Fruity Dippers

INGREDIENTS

serves ❶ to ❷

2 oz/55 g raspberries

1 tsp orange juice

2 tbsp plain or strained plain yogurt

CHOOSE FROM FRUITS,
SUCH AS:

½ small banana, cut into chunks

½ apple, peeled and cut into long slices

½ pear, peeled and cut into long slices

3–4 seedless grapes, halved

1 oz/25 g mango, cut into long thin slices

½ peach or nectarine, cut into slices

½ kiwi, cut into sticks

1 To make the dip, press the raspberries through a nylon strainer to remove the seeds. Stir the raspberry puree and orange juice into the yogurt and spoon into a small dish. Arrange the fruits on a plate with the dip.

Apple Fritters

INGREDIENTS

serves ❹

corn oil, for deep-frying

1 large egg

pinch of salt

¾ cup water

⅜ cup all-purpose flour

2 tsp ground cinnamon

heaping ¼ cup superfine sugar

4 apples, peeled and cored

1 Pour the corn oil into a deep fryer or large, heavy-bottom pan and heat to 350–375°F/ 180–190°C, or until a cube of bread browns in 30 seconds.

2 Meanwhile, using an electric mixer, beat the egg and salt together until frothy, then quickly whisk in the water and flour. Do not overbeat the batter—it doesn't matter if it isn't completely smooth.

3 Mix the cinnamon and sugar together in a shallow dish and set aside.

4 Slice the apples into ¼-inch/5-mm thick rings. Spear with a fork, 1 slice at a time, and dip in the batter to coat. Add to the hot oil, in batches, and cook for 1 minute on each side, or until golden and puffed up. Remove with a slotted spoon and drain on paper towels. Keep warm while you cook the remaining batches. Transfer to a large serving plate, sprinkle with the cinnamon sugar, and serve.

Chocolate Popcorn

INGREDIENTS

3 tbsp sunflower oil

¼ cup popcorn

2 tbsp butter

¼ cup light brown sugar

2 tbsp dark corn syrup

1 tbsp milk

2 oz/55 g semisweet dark
chocolate chips

serves 6 to 8

1 Preheat the oven to 300°F/150°C. Heat the oil in a large, heavy-bottom pan. Add the popcorn kernels, cover the pan, and cook, shaking the pan vigorously and frequently, for about 2 minutes, until the popping stops. Turn into a large bowl.

2 Put the butter, sugar, corn syrup, and milk in a pan and heat gently until the butter has melted. Bring to a boil, without stirring, and boil for 2 minutes. Remove from the heat, add the chocolate chips, and stir until melted.

3 Pour the chocolate mixture over the popcorn and toss together until evenly coated. Spread the mixture onto a large cookie sheet.

4 Bake the popcorn in the oven for about 15 minutes, until crisp. Let cool before serving.

Oat Bars

INGREDIENTS

makes 16

¾ cup unsalted butter, plus extra for greasing

3 tbsp honey

heaping ¾ cup packed raw sugar

3½ oz/100 g no-added-sugar smooth peanut butter

2¾ cups oatmeal

heaping ¼ cup plumped dried apricots, chopped

2 tbsp sunflower seeds

2 tbsp sesame seeds

1 Preheat the oven to 350°F/180°C. Grease and line an 8½-inch/22-cm square baking pan.

2 Melt the butter, honey, and sugar in a pan over low heat. When the sugar has melted, add the peanut butter, and stir until all the ingredients are well combined. Add all the remaining ingredients and mix well.

3 Press the mixture into the prepared pan and bake in the preheated oven for 20 minutes.

4 Remove from the oven and let cool in the pan, then cut into 16 squares.

6 Treats

Children love a dessert or snack as a treat and this chapter gives you plenty of ideas. Cutting cakes and cookies into shapes, such as stars or people, will always attract youngsters, as does food that can be eaten easily with the fingers. Skewered fruit kebabs are ideal, and an excellent way of encouraging your children to eat fruit. Ice cream with whole strawberries or a gleaming strawberry sauce makes an extra-special treat for a birthday.

Apricot & Sunflower Seed Cookies

INGREDIENTS

serves 6 to 8

7 tbsp unsalted butter, softened

¼ cup packed raw sugar

1 tbsp maple syrup

1 tbsp honey, plus extra for brushing

1 large egg, beaten

scant ¾ cup white all-purpose flour, plus extra for dusting

scant 1½ cups whole wheat all-purpose flour

1 tbsp oat bran

½ cup ground almonds

1 tsp ground cinnamon

½ cup plumped dried apricots, chopped

2 tbsp sunflower seeds

1 Beat the softened butter with the sugar in a large bowl until light and fluffy. Beat in the maple syrup and honey, then the egg.

2 Add the flours and oat bran, then the almonds and mix well. Add the cinnamon, apricots, and seeds and, with floured hands, mix to a firm dough. Wrap in plastic wrap and let chill for 30 minutes.

3 Preheat the oven to 350°F/180°C. Roll out the dough on a lightly floured counter to ½-inch/ 1 cm thick. Using a 2½-inch/6-cm cookie cutter, cut out 20 circles, rerolling the trimmings where possible, and place on a baking sheet. Brush with a little extra honey and bake in the preheated oven for 15 minutes, until golden. Remove from the oven and let cool on a wire rack.

Orange & Banana Biscuits

INGREDIENTS

sunflower oil, for oiling

heaping 1 cup white
self-rising flour, plus extra
for dusting, and rolling
if needed

heaping 1 cup whole wheat
self-rising flour

1 tsp baking powder

½ tsp ground cinnamon

generous 5½ tbsp unsalted
butter, diced and chilled

¼ cup packed brown sugar

⅔ cup whole milk, plus extra
for brushing

1 ripe banana, peeled and
mashed

finely grated rind of 1 orange

1¼ cups fresh raspberries,
lightly mashed

makes ❶❷

1 Preheat the oven to 400°F/200°C. Lightly oil a large baking sheet.

2 Mix the flours, baking powder, and cinnamon together in a large bowl, add the butter, and rub in with your fingertips until the mixture resembles breadcrumbs. Stir in the sugar. Make a well in the middle and pour in the milk, add the banana and orange rind, and mix to a soft dough. The dough will be wet.

3 Turn out the dough onto a lightly floured counter and, adding a little more flour if needed, roll out to ¾ inch/2 cm thick. Using a 2½-inch/6-cm cookie cutter, cut out 12 biscuits, rerolling the trimmings where possible, and place them on the prepared baking sheet. Brush with milk and bake in the preheated oven for 10–12 minutes.

4 Remove from the oven and let cool slightly, then halve the biscuits and fill with the raspberries.

Gingerbread People

INGREDIENTS

1¼ cups all-purpose flour

2 tsp ground ginger

½ tsp baking soda

4 tbsp butter or margarine

scant ½ cup brown sugar

2 tbsp dark corn syrup

1 egg, beaten

TO DECORATE

sugar-coated chocolate candies and jelly orange and lemon cake decorations

makes ❹ people or more, depending on the size

1 Preheat the oven to 375°F/190°C. Sift the flour, ginger and baking soda into a large mixing bowl. Add the butter and rub into the flour with your fingertips until it resembles fine breadcrumbs. Mix in the sugar.

2 Warm the syrup in a small saucepan until runny, then add to the flour mixture with the beaten egg. Mix to form a soft dough, then knead lightly until smooth. If the dough is too sticky, add a little extra flour.

3 Roll out the dough on a lightly floured counter then, using a cutter, make the gingerbread people. Place on a lightly greased baking sheet and cook for 10 minutes, or until just crisp and golden. Let cool.

4 Use the chocolate candies to make eyes and buttons, and attach the jelly orange and lemon cake decorations to make a mouth.

Apple & Blueberry with Oaty Cobbler Topping

INGREDIENTS

7 oz/200 g mixed apple and blueberries

pinch of ground cinnamon

1 tsp superfine sugar

COBBLER TOPPING

⅓ cup all-purpose flour

½ tsp baking powder

2 tsp superfine sugar

1 oz/25 g unsalted butter

¼ cup sour cream

1 tbsp rolled oats

serves ❷

1 Preheat the oven to 400°F/200°C. Put the fruit, cinnamon, and sugar into a small saucepan with 1 tablespoon water. Heat gently and cook for a few minutes until the fruit begins to soften. Remove from the heat.

2 Divide the fruit between two individual ovenproof dishes. Put the flour, baking powder, sugar, and butter into a small bowl and rub in until the mixture resembles fresh breadcrumbs. Mix in the sour cream. Put the rolled oats on to a saucer, then drop teaspoonfuls of the mixture on top and roll in the oats. Flatten the pieces slightly and arrange on top of the fruit. Put the dishes on a baking sheet and bake for about 20 minutes, until golden brown.

Fragrant Rice Dessert

INGREDIENTS

⅓ cup short-grain rice

1¼ cups whole milk

seeds from 1 cardamom pod, crushed

½ tsp vanilla extract

2 tsp sugar (optional)

milk or orange juice, for thinning (optional)

1 large orange, peel and pith removed and cut into segments

1 tsp clear honey

few drops of orange flower water

serves ❷ to ❸

1 Put the rice, milk, crushed cardamom seeds, vanilla extract, and sugar, if using, into a small saucepan. Bring to a boil and simmer very gently for about 20 minutes, stirring frequently. When the rice grains are very soft, remove from the heat and let cool. Thin with a little milk or orange juice if necessary.

2 Put the orange segments into a dish and drizzle over the honey and orange flower water. Toss gently together and serve with the rice pudding.

Ice Cream with Strawberry Sauce & Star Cookies

INGREDIENTS

serves 8 to 10

2½ cups heavy cream

1 vanilla pod, split

4 egg yolks

¼ cup superfine sugar

6 oz/175 g strawberries

1 tbsp confectioners' sugar

STAR COOKIES

½ cup confectioners' sugar, sifted

6 tbsp unsalted butter, softened

1 egg yolk

1 cup all-purpose flour, plus extra for dusting

1 Put the cream into a saucepan. Scrape the seeds from the vanilla pod and add them to the saucepan, together with the pod. Bring to a boil, remove from the heat, and let stand for about 20 minutes.

2 Mix together the egg yolks and superfine sugar. Pour on the cream. Return the mixture to the cleaned saucepan and cook very gently until the mixture starts to thicken, stirring constantly. Pour through a strainer into a bowl. Cover and let stand until cold.

3 Churn the mixture in an ice-cream maker, or pour into a bowl and freeze. When it is half frozen, remove and whisk. Return to the freezer. Repeat 4 or 5 times.

4 To make the sauce, put the strawberries and confectioners' sugar into a bowl and puree using a handheld mixer.

5 To make the star cookies, preheat the oven to 350°F/180°C. Put all the ingredients into a bowl and mix until a smooth dough is formed. Roll out on a floured surface and cut out small star shapes. Place on a nonstick baking sheet and bake for 5–10 minutes, until golden brown. Serve the ice cream with the sauce and the star cookies.

Baby Baked Apples with Fudge Yogurt

INGREDIENTS

scant 1 cup heavy cream

scant 1 cup drained plain yogurt

4 tbsp dark brown sugar

4 small apples

8 plumped dried apricots, chopped

2 tsp butter

serves 4

1 To make the fudge yogurt, whisk the heavy cream until thick. Fold in the yogurt and put into a bowl. Sprinkle over the brown sugar, then cover and chill in the refrigerator for 1 hour. During chilling, the sugar will liquefy and form a thin layer of "sauce."

2 Preheat the oven to 400°F/200°C.

3 Wash the apples and remove the cores. Using a sharp knife, make an incision around each apple about halfway up, so the apple can expand during baking. Put the apples in a small ovenproof dish and fill the apples with the apricots. Put a pat of butter on top of each one and bake in the oven for about 15 minutes, or until soft.

4 Swirl the liquefied sugar through the yogurt and serve with the warm apples.

Sugar-Frosted Fruit Pie

INGREDIENTS

serves 6

scant 2½ cups self-raising flour

¾ cup butter

water, for mixing and brushing

1 tbsp cornstarch

3½ oz/100 g superfine sugar

1 tsp ground cinnamon

finely grated rind of 1 small orange

finely grated rind of 1 small lemon

8 Granny Smith apples, peeled, cored and sliced

2 tsp lemon juice

cream, ice cream, or custard, to serve

TOPPING

1 egg white, beaten until frothy

1 tbsp superfine sugar

1 Preheat the oven to 400°F/200°C. Place a baking sheet in the oven.

2 Put the flour into a bowl and rub in the butter until the mixture resembles fine breadcrumbs. Add enough water to mix to a soft but not sticky dough. Roll out just under half the dough on a floured surface and use to line the bottom of a 9-inch/22-cm pie plate.

3 Mix together the cornstarch, sugar, cinnamon, and orange and lemon rinds and toss together with the apples and lemon juice. Pile the mixture into the pastry-lined dish. Dampen the edge of the pastry with water. Roll out the remaining pastry and use to cover the pie. Roll out any trimmings and cut out leaf shapes. Brush these with water and attach them to the pie. Brush the top of the pie with beaten egg white and sprinkle with sugar. Place the pie on the hot baking sheet in the oven and cook for about 30–40 minutes, until golden brown. Serve with cream, ice cream, or custard.

Chocolate Mousse

INGREDIENTS

makes 6

3½ oz/100 g semisweet chocolate (minimum 70% cocoa solids), chopped

1 tbsp butter

2 large eggs, separated

1 tbsp maple syrup

2 tbsp strained plain yogurt

heaping ½ cup blueberries

1 tbsp water

1 oz/25 g white chocolate, grated

1 Put the chocolate and butter in a heatproof bowl, set the bowl over a pan of barely simmering water, and heat until melted. Let cool slightly, then stir in the egg yolks, maple syrup, and yogurt.

2 Whisk the egg whites in a large, grease-free bowl until stiff, then fold into the chocolate mixture. Divide between 6 small bowls or glasses and let chill for 4 hours.

3 Meanwhile, put the blueberries in a small pan with the water and cook until the berries begin to pop and turn glossy. Let cool, then let chill.

4 To serve, top each mousse with a few blueberries and a little white chocolate.

Strawberry Yogurt Popsicles

INGREDIENTS

350 g/12 oz fresh strawberries, hulled and sliced

1¼ cups thick plain yogurt

3 tbsp honey

few drops of vanilla extract

makes ❻

1 Put the strawberries, yogurt, honey, and vanilla extract in a blender and process until smooth.

2 Pour the mixture into popsicle-style molds and freeze until solid. (Fun-shaped molds are popular.)

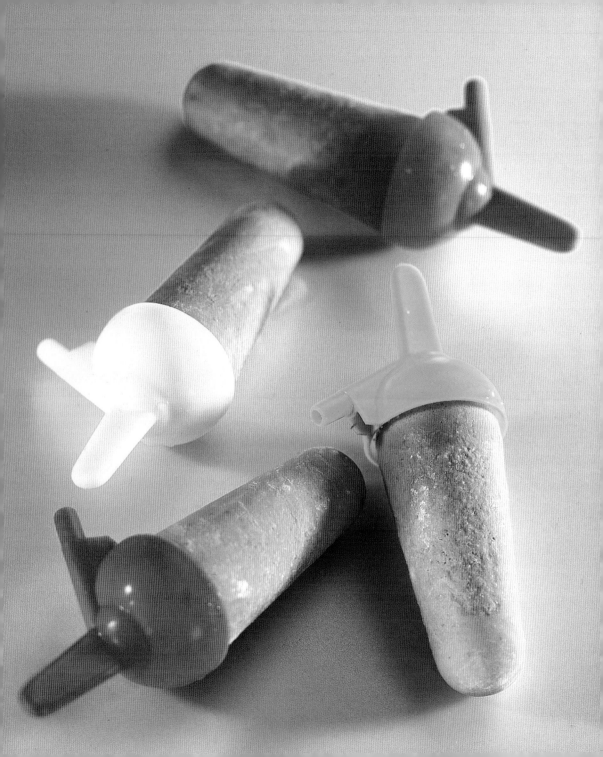

Mini Strawberry Cheesecakes

INGREDIENTS

makes 6

generous 5½ tbsp unsalted butter

scant 1 cup rolled oats

heaping 2 tbsp chopped hazelnuts

1 cup ricotta cheese

¼ cup packed brown sugar

finely grated rind of 1 lemon, and juice of ½ lemon

1 egg, plus 1 egg yolk

scant ¾ cup cottage cheese

1 kiwi

6 large strawberries

1 Line 6 holes of a muffin pan with muffin paper cases.

2 Melt the butter in a small pan over low heat, then let cool. Put the oats in a food processor and blend briefly to break them up, then put into a bowl, add the nuts and melted butter, and mix well. Divide the mixture between the paper cases and press down well. Let chill for 30 minutes.

3 Preheat the oven to 300°F/150°C. Beat the ricotta cheese with the sugar and lemon rind and juice in a bowl. Add the egg, egg yolk, and cottage cheese and mix well. Spoon into the muffin cases and bake in the preheated oven for 30 minutes. Turn off the oven, but let the cheesecakes stand in the oven until completely cold.

4 Peel the kiwi and dice the flesh, and slice the strawberries. Remove the paper cases, top each cheesecake with the fruit, and serve.

Ice Cream Strawberry Sundae

INGREDIENTS

serves 4

8 scoops of good-quality vanilla ice cream

¼ cup chopped mixed nuts, lightly toasted in a dry skillet

grated chocolate and marshmallows, to serve

STRAWBERRY SAUCE

9 oz/250 g strawberries, hulled and halved

2 tbsp freshly squeezed orange juice

2 tbsp superfine sugar

1 To make the sauce, put the strawberries in a blender with the orange juice and process until smooth. Transfer the mixture to a saucepan and add the sugar. Cook over a medium heat for 10–12 minutes, or until thickened. Let cool.

2 To serve, place a spoonful of the strawberry sauce in the bottom of a tall glass. Add two scoops of ice cream and another spoonful of fruit sauce. Sprinkle with the nuts and chocolate. Arrange the marshmallows on top. Repeat to make four sundaes.

Fruit Skewers

INGREDIENTS

selection of fruit, such as apricots, peaches, figs, strawberries, mangoes, pineapple, bananas, dates, and papaya, prepared and cut into chunks

MAPLE SYRUP

1¾ oz/50 g semisweet dark chocolate (minimum 70% cocoa solids), broken into chunks

makes ❹

1 Soak 4 bamboo fruit skewers in water for at least 20 minutes.

2 Preheat the broiler to high and line the broiler pan with foil. Thread alternate pieces of fruit onto each skewer. Brush the fruit with a little maple syrup.

3 Put the chocolate in a heatproof bowl, set the bowl over a pan of barely simmering water, and heat until it is melted.

4 Meanwhile, cook the fruit skewers under the preheated broiler for 3 minutes, or until caramelized. Serve drizzled with a little of the melted chocolate, removing the fruit from the skewer if serving to younger children.

Index

apples
apple & blueberry with oaty
cobbler topping 156
apple & hazelnut bread 28
apple fritters 142
baby baked apples with
fudge yogurt 162
chicken & apple bites 52
sugar-frosted fruit pie 164
apricots
apricot & sunflower seed
cookies 150
muesli muffins 12
oat bars 146
avocado
avocado dip with spicy
potato skins 132
chicken & avocado sandwich
filling 122
green fingers 128

bananas
malted banana smoothie 14
orange & banana biscuits 152
waffles with caramelized
bananas 32
beans and pulses
bean burgers 116
hearty bean & pasta soup 102
hummus with crunchy
vegetables 124
nachos 138
Tex-Mex roll ups 60
beef
brilliant hamburgers 42
mini meatballs & spaghetti 38
shepherd's pie 44
spaghetti Bolognese 40
blueberries
apple & blueberry with oaty
cobbler topping 156
blueberry bran muffins 20
broccoli: creamy smoked salmon &
broccoli pasta 80
burgers
bean burgers 116
brilliant hamburgers 42

cheese
baked eggs with ham &
tomato 30
broiled cheese sandwich 126
cheese twists 130
cheesy corn fritters 110
chicken quesadilla triangles 58
creamy smoked salmon &
broccoli pasta 80
crispy vegetable bake 118
fruity cheese spread 122
ham & pineapple muffin
pizzas 134
ham pizza 46
herbed vegetable & pasta
cheese 96
mini strawberry
cheesecakes 170
nachos 138
perfect pasta 48
roast vegetable lasagna 114
Tex-Mex roll ups 60

vegetable lasagna 100
chicken
chicken & apple bites 52
chicken & avocado sandwich
filling 122
chicken quesadilla triangles 58
chicken satay bites 54
homemade chicken nuggets 50
oven-fried chicken wings 136
sticky drumsticks &
cucumber salad 62
surf 'n' turf paella 88
sweet & sour chicken
stir-fry 56
Tex-Mex roll ups 60
chickpeas: hummus with
crunchy vegetables 124
chocolate
chocolate mousse 166
chocolate popcorn 144
coconut
coconut muesli 16
shrimp with coconut rice 90
cod
fish pie 84
homemade fish sticks &
sweet potato wedges 72
sunny rice 86
corn
cheesy corn fritters 110
chocolate popcorn 144
tortillas with tuna, egg, &
corn 68
tuna & corn sandwich
filling 122
cucumber: sticky drumsticks &
cucumber salad 62

eggs
baked egg with ham &
tomato 30
baked eggs 18
Chinese rice with omelet
strips 108
crispy vegetable bake 118
deep-pan omelet 112
fish pie 84
salmon with egg-fried
rice 78
sunny rice 86
sunshine toast 22
tortillas with tuna, egg, &
corn 68

fruit
fruit skewers 174
fruit smoothie 14
fruity cheese spread 122
fruity dippers 140
fruity maple porridge 34
fruity purple oatmeal 10

gingerbread people 154
guacamole 128

haddock: see smoked haddock
ham
baked egg with ham &
tomato 30
broiled cheese sandwich 126

ham & pineapple muffin
pizzas 134
ham pizza 46
perfect pasta 48
honey salmon kebabs 82
hummus with crunchy
vegetables 124

ice cream
ice cream strawberry sundae 172
ice cream with strawberry
sauce & star cookies 160

lamb: shepherd's pie 44

muesli
coconut muesli 16
muesli muffins 12

nachos 138
noodles: Chinese noodles 98
nuts
apple & hazelnut bread 28
Bircher granola 26
coconut muesli 16
crunchy yogurt 24

oats
apple & blueberry with oaty
cobbler topping 156
Bircher granola 26
crunchy yogurt 24
fruity maple porridge 34
fruity purple oatmeal 10
mini strawberry
cheesecakes 170
oat bars 146
oranges
fragrant rice dessert 158
orange & banana biscuits 152

pasta
creamy smoked salmon &
broccoli pasta 80
hearty bean & pasta soup 102
herbed vegetable & pasta
cheese 96
minestrone soup 94
mini meatballs & spaghetti 38
perfect pasta 48
roast vegetable lasagna 114
spaghetti Bolognese 40
tuna & pasta salad 66
two-fish casserole 74
vegetable lasagna 100
warm pasta salad 106
peanut butter
chicken satay bites 54
oat bars 146
pineapple
ham & pineapple muffin
pizzas 134
sweet & sour chicken
stir-fry 56
potatoes
avocado dip with spicy
potato skins 132
crispy vegetable bake 118
deep-pan omelet 112
salmon cakes 76

shepherd's pie 44
rice
Chinese rice with omelet
strips 108
fragrant rice dessert 158
salmon with egg-fried rice 78
shrimp with coconut rice 90
sunny rice 86
surf 'n' turf paella 88
salmon
creamy smoked salmon &
broccoli pasta 80
honey salmon kebabs 82
salmon cakes 76
salmon with egg-fried rice 78
sandwich fillings 122
shrimp
shrimp with coconut rice 90
surf 'n' turf paella 88
smoked haddock
fish pie 84
sunny rice 86
two-fish casserole 74
smoothies 14
strawberries
ice cream strawberry
sundae 172
ice cream with strawberry
sauce & star cookies 160
mini strawberry
cheesecakes 170
strawberry yogurt
popsicles 168
sunflower seeds: apricot &
sunflower seed
cookies 150
sweet potatoes
homemade fish sticks &
sweet potato wedges 72
shepherd's pie 44

tofu: Chinese noodles 98
tomatoes
baked egg with ham &
tomato 30
creamy tomato soup 104
minestrone soup 94
mini meatballs & spaghetti 38
spaghetti Bolognese 40
tuna
tortillas with tuna, egg, &
corn 68
tuna & corn sandwich
filling 122
tuna & pasta salad 66
tuna bites 70

vegetables
crispy vegetable bake 118
herbed vegetable & pasta
cheese 96
roast vegetable lasagna 114
vegetable lasagna 100

yogurt
baby baked apples with
fudge yogurt 162
crunchy yogurt 24
strawberry yogurt
popsicles 168